SAINT FRANCES CABRINI

Catholic Story Coloring Book

This is her story, written by Mary Fabyan Windeatt
With pictures for you to color, drawn by Gedge Harmon

This book belongs to

_____

*The pictures in this book can be colored
with crayons, markers or water colors.*

TAN BOOKS AND PUBLISHERS, INC., ROCKFORD, ILLINOIS 61105

CHAPTER ONE

IT was a bright summer day in the year 1858 as Father Louis Oldini set out from his rectory in Livagra (a village in northern Italy near the town of Lodi), with a favorite young visitor by the hand.

"Well, Francie, where are we going today?" he demanded jovially. "Surely not down to the river again?"

Eight-year-old Mary Frances Cabrini nodded eagerly. "Oh, yes, Uncle Louis! Please!"

"But we were there yesterday, child. And the day before, too."

"I know. But I want to sail my boats, and the river's the only place."

The priest chuckled. This young niece from nearby Sant' Angelo surely had a way with her. "Very well, my dear," he said cheerfully. "It's down to the river again. I'll read my Office while you sail your boats."

Soon the little girl was happily lost in play. What did it matter if her boats were only paper ones piled high with violets from along the river bank? She would pretend the flowers were missionaries, and that the boats would take them safely down the swift waters of the Venera all the way to China.

"Some day I'll be going to China, too," she mused happily. "Some day I'll be telling all the little pagan children there about Jesus."

SAINT FRANCES CABRINI

CHAPTER TWO

FRANCES' oldest sister Rose (who taught school in Sant' Angelo), only laughed at such a plan. "You, a missionary?" she scoffed one night. "Nonsense, child! You're much too frail for the religious life."

Twelve-year-old Francie lowered her eyes. She was the youngest of the thirteen Cabrini children and had always obeyed Rose as readily as her parents. But surely this time—

"Some day I'll be big and strong," she protested. "Just wait and see."

"So? And then what'll you do?"

"Why, I'll enter a convent, and ask the Sisters to let me work in China."

Rose's lips tightened. Was Francie growing up to be a stubborn young girl who wouldn't take anyone's advice? Worse still, was she beginning to be proud of her extraordinary good looks—the deep blue eyes and golden curls which set her apart from every other youngster in Sant' Angelo?

"Bring me your brush and comb," she ordered grimly.

The child looked up in surprise. "My brush and comb?"

"You heard me. I'm going to straighten out those silly curls of yours once and for all."

Trying not to be hurt at the harshness in her sister's voice, Francie hastened to obey. Poor Rose! What a hard day she must have had in school to be so cross tonight!

SAINT FRANCES CABRINI

CHAPTER THREE

AUGUSTINE and Stella Cabrini often marveled at their youngest child's fondness for her overbearing sister. "The little one's an angel," declared Augustine one day. "She never complains about a thing. But what's to become of her when we're gone, Stella? After all, we do have to think about the future, you know."

The mother smiled. "Francie still wants to be a nun, dear."

"A nun! What convent would have the poor child when she's so small and frail? No, she'd do better to stay in the world and be a schoolteacher like Rose."

Since the pastor of Sant' Angelo was of like mind, thirteen-year-old Mary Frances Cabrini finally entered the boarding school of the Daughters of the Sacred Heart at Arluno to study for her teacher's diploma.

"I know the Sisters will let me join them when I've finished my studies," she told herself confidently. "Then some day, when they open a school in China, they'll let me go there to work."

But in 1868, when the teacher's diploma was finally hers, eighteen-year-old Frances faced her parents tearfully. "Oh, Mama! Papa! Reverend Mother says I'm not called to the religious life! She...she just won't have me at all!"

Stella reached out her arms. "There, child, don't worry," she said tenderly. "Surely the good God knows what's best for us?"

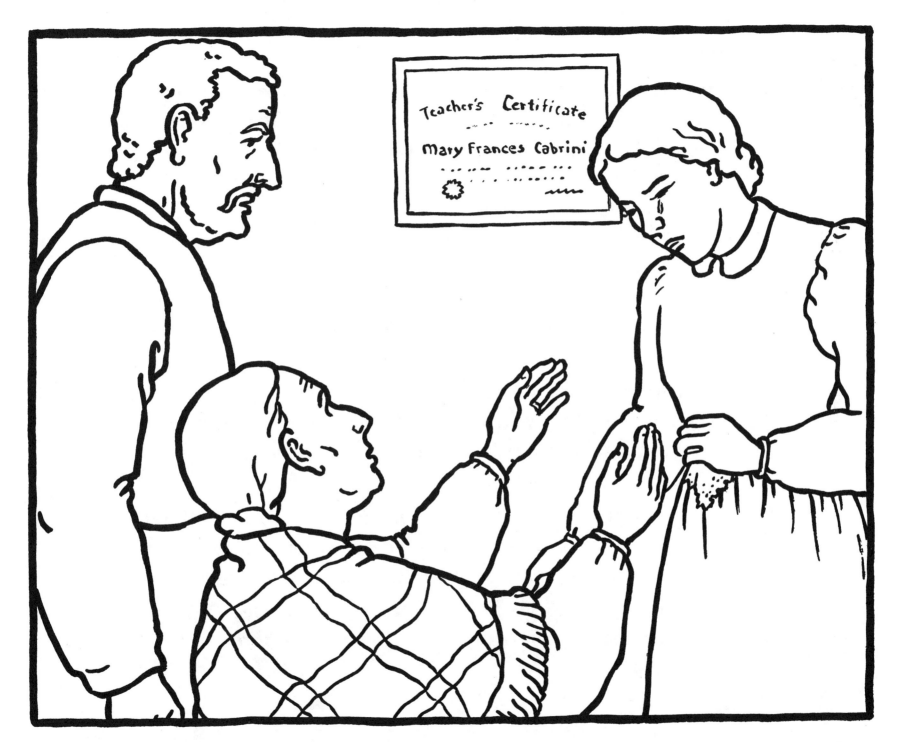

The certificate reads: Teacher's Certificate — Mary Frances Cabrini

SAINT FRANCES CABRINI

CHAPTER FOUR

DURING the next six years (which were divided between working at home and teaching in the nearby village of Vidardo), Frances often recalled her mother's words. Yes, it was foolish to worry about the future. That belonged to God for Him to do with as He pleased.

"You're a very wise young woman," said Monsignor Serrati, the pastor at Vidardo, when Frances voiced this thought to him. "But now let's see if you really mean what you say."

"Why, Monsignor—"

"In a few weeks I'm being transferred to Codogno. In my opinion, it's God's Will that you come there to teach at the orphanage for girls."

Twenty-four-year-old Frances stared in amazement. What could she do at the orphanage when it was already in charge of three women much older than herself? Women who had taken vows, and were now leading the religious life?

"Monsignor, you're joking!"

"No, my dear, I'm not. Those women in Codogno mean well, but things are going from bad to worse at the orphanage because they don't know how to manage young girls. But if you could help to organize a few classes—"

Finally Frances agreed to go to Codogno for two weeks. Yes, she would do what she could for the orphan girls, as well as for the three women who were trying to train them.

SAINT FRANCES CABRINI

CHAPTER FIVE

FRANCES' work at Codogno was so successful that Monsignor Serrati finally prevailed upon her to join the three women at the orphanage as a religious. What did it matter that she had wanted to serve God as a missionary to China? She could work for Him in Italy just as well. The Bishop agreed with the Monsignor, and six years later (during which time Frances had been named superior at the orphanage), he made a surprising suggestion.

"Mother, you've always wanted to be a missionary," he said, smiling, "but I know of no missionary Order for women in the Church. Now, why don't you found one yourself?"

Mother Cabrini's heart beat fast. What a wonderful idea! "I'll look for a house right away," she said quickly. "Thank you, Your Lordship! Thank you so much!"

By November 14 of that same year, 1880, Mother Cabrini and seven companions (who some day would be known as the Missionary Sisters of the Sacred Heart), were happily established in new quarters in Codogno. And though for the time being their work would be the education of young girls, surely it would eventually extend to many other fields as well?

"Dear Lord, do let us work for You in China!" pleaded the thirty-year-old superior as she knelt in the little chapel before a picture of the Sacred Heart. "Please do!"

SAINT FRANCES CABRINI

CHAPTER SIX

ALTHOUGH her new convent was very poor, Mother Cabrini made it self-supporting. Every student was taught to cook, sew and embroider. Indeed, when two years had passed, word of the Sisters' young needleworkers' skill had spread to Grumello, a small town near the city of Cremona, and a second school had to be opened. Two years later, in Milan, a third school came into being.

Monsignor Serrati scarcely knew what to think. How had Mother Frances Cabrini managed to accomplish so much? Now thirty-four years old, she was as small and frail as ever. Often she was confined to bed with such pains and fever that every breath seemed to be her last. Yet a few days later she would be up and around again, busy with exciting new plans for her growing community.

"It's a miracle, Your Lordship," he confided to the Bishop one day. "Don't you agree?"

The Bishop nodded thoughtfully. "I do. And not the first one either. After all, remember how the Sisters were short of bread last week, with not a cent in the house to buy more? And when they told Mother Cabrini about it, and she had prayed, the cook suddenly found a supply of good fresh loaves in the bin?"

The Monsignor smiled. "Yes, Your Lordship. But Mother Cabrini says—"

"That the cook didn't look carefully in the bin in the first place? Nonsense! We have a saint in our midst, my friend. A truly great servant of God."

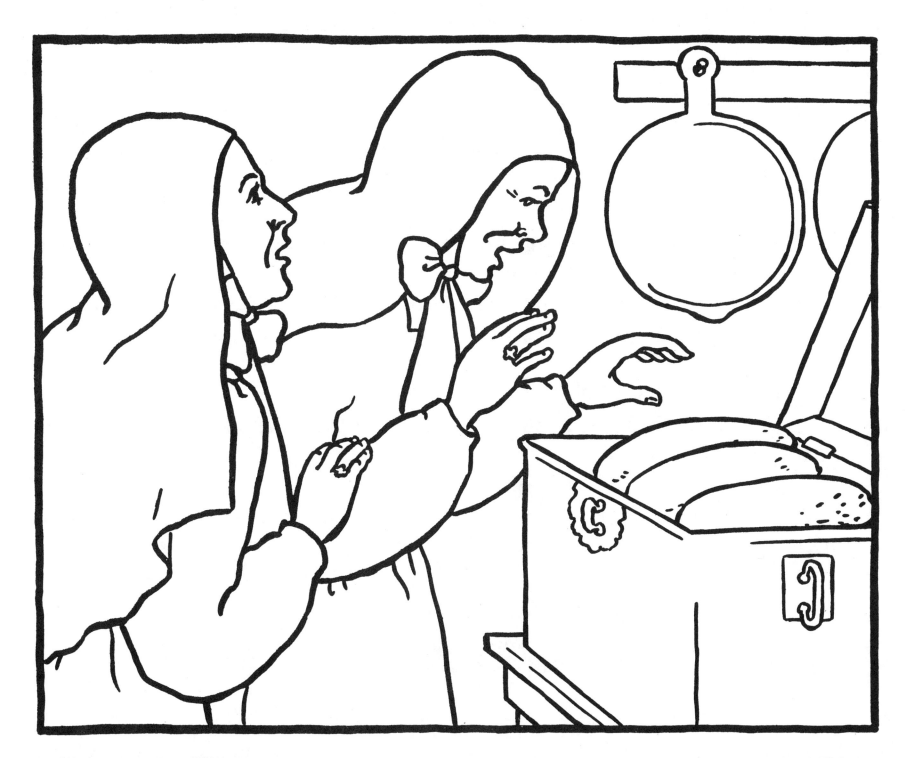

CHAPTER SEVEN

IN 1887, after Mother Cabrini had prayed long and hard to receive permission from the Holy Father to begin missionary work in China, a certain Bishop Scalabrini had an inspiration. "Mother, you'd better work for souls in the United States than anywhere else," he declared bluntly. "Believe me, I know what I'm talking about."

Mother Cabrini nodded politely. The Bishop had just written a book on the plight of the Italian immigrant in the New World. And though everything in the book was true—the terrible awakening of the thousands of Italians who had come to America believing the streets were paved with gold—the poverty, the heartbreak, the final drifting away from God and His Church—surely these problems were no special concern of hers?

"Yes, Your Lordship, things must be very hard for the poor immigrants," she admitted readily, "especially when they can't speak English, or find suitable employment. On the other hand—"

"On the other hand, you and your Sisters can easily change the whole picture, Mother. You can open a school for Italian children in New York, persuade the parents to have faith in God and return to the Sacraments—"

"But China, Your Lordship! For years my heart's been set on going there!"

The Bishop smiled. "Yes, Mother, I know. But I also know it may be God's Will that you go west, not east, in His service."

SAINT FRANCES CABRINI

CHAPTER EIGHT

POPE Leo the Thirteenth agreed with Bishop Scalabrini, and late in March of the year 1889 Mother Cabrini sailed from the French port of Le Havre to begin missionary work among the Italian population of New York. Scarcely had the S.S. Bourgogne left the dock, however, than her six companions began to experience all the terrible agony of seasickness.

"Oh, Mother, I'm dying!"

"The boat's going down, Mother!"

"We'll never see New York at all!"

"Or have a decent grave!"

Mother Cabrini could hardly keep from laughing. True, there were few luxuries on the Bourgogne—a creaking old vessel that would take many days to cross the Atlantic—but so far the weather was favorable and she herself felt like a new person in the bracing sea air.

"Nonsense, my dears, everything's going to be all right," she said soothingly. "You're just tired and frightened."

The Sisters tried to believe this, but soon all had taken to their beds, convinced that the end had come. And when, in mid-Atlantic, a stiff gale sprang up and the Bourgogne began to roll and toss in a dangerous sea—

"Oh, Mother, how can you stand it?"

"It's too horrible, Mother! It really is!"

SAINT FRANCES CABRINI

CHAPTER NINE

ONCE the group was settled in New York, however, past hardships were quickly forgotten. How much work there was to be done in the slums of the lower East Side where hundreds of Italian families were drifting away from the Church!

"It's just as Bishop Scalabrini said," Mother Cabrini told her little community. "Through poverty and ignorance, without enough Italian-speaking priests to guide them, our good people are like lost sheep in this New World. Now, though, with God's help—"

"We'll open a school, Mother?"

"Yes, my dears. And an orphanage, too."

To the amazement of everyone, including Archbishop Corrigan of New York, both projects were accomplished within just a few weeks. The school was in Saint Joachim's Church, on the lower East Side, the orphanage on East Fifty-ninth Street. And since money, food and clothing were badly needed, a daily begging tour was promptly organized in both neighborhoods.

There were difficulties, of course, but Mother Cabrini's courage never faltered. Since the Vicar of Christ on earth, Pope Leo the Thirteenth, had sent her to the New World, surely her work there would be blessed?

"Sisters, a missionary should never be afraid to try the impossible," she declared, smiling, "especially a Missionary Sister of the Sacred Heart."

SAINT FRANCES CABRINI

CHAPTER TEN

BY July, 1890, just sixteen months after she had come to the United States, Mother Cabrini had made many new friends. And not only among the poor Italians of New York's lower East Side, but among more prosperous folk as well.

"Mother, you handle money matters better than I do," chuckled a certain lawyer one day. "First, you open a school and orphanage on little more than pennies. Now you buy Manresa, the Jesuits' beautiful estate up the Hudson river. Tell me, how do you explain all this success?"

Mother Cabrini's blue eyes sparkled. "God has been very good, sir. And the Jesuit Fathers, too. They let us have Manresa as a real bargain."

"Some bargain, considering that it had no good water supply!"

"But sir! Haven't you heard? Last week, after we had prayed long and hard to Our Lady, we decided to try our luck at digging a well at Manresa. And in no time at all—"

"You found water?"

"Yes, sir. Plenty of fresh, clear water. Oh, I'm so happy about it! Manresa will make a grand home for our orphans."

For a moment the lawyer was thoughtful. Could it be that the prayers of Mother Frances Cabrini were extraordinarily powerful with God? That this little Italian nun—so frail, yet possessed of boundless energy—was actually a saint?

SAINT FRANCES CABRINI

CHAPTER ELEVEN

SOON other people were asking the same questions. For not only had Mother Cabrini done wonders for her fellow-countrymen since her arrival in New York. Now, with a group of Sisters from the Motherhouse in Codogno, she was on her way to open a girls' school in Nicaragua. Even more. In just a few months she would be back in the United States to establish a house in New Orleans and a hospital in New York.

"Only a saint could do so much good for so many people in such a short time," one person told another wonderingly.

"That's right. And a great saint at that."

"But of course Mother Cabrini doesn't like to be called a saint."

"Oh, no! It bothers her dreadfully."

Mother Cabrini was uncomfortable when well-meaning friends suggested she was something of a wonderworker. If her present labors were being blessed, she said, if money and vocations were coming in from the most unexpected sources, surely it was only because of the act of faith she had made in obeying the Holy Father's command that she go west instead of east in a search for souls?

"To become perfect, all you have to do is to obey perfectly," she told her little orphans one day. "Do you understand, my dears?"

The children nodded eagerly. "Oh, yes, Mother! You explained all about that the last time you were here."

SAINT FRANCES CABRINI

CHAPTER TWELVE

BY September, 1892, the Missionary Sisters in New York were hard at work in their new Columbus Hospital—so named to honor the four hundredth anniversary of the great Italian explorer's discovery of America. And though this was only a shabby tenement on East Twelfth Street, with room for scarcely a dozen patients, Mother Cabrini felt sure the work there would prosper.

"I'll ask the Holy Father to pray for this intention," she told her Sisters cheerfully. "Also, that soon we'll be able to start work in South America."

The Sisters looked at one another doubtfully. Besides the trip to Nicaragua last year and the more recent visit to New Orleans, Mother Cabrini had twice returned to Italy to secure more vocations to the missionary life. And though so far her frail health had stood up under the constant strain, it surely would be unwise to add to the burden? Especially when the community's chief work still lay among the underprivileged Italians in New York?

"But Saint Joachim's school, Mother!"

"The orphanage at Manresa!"

"And now our hospital! Oh, don't you think we have enough work to do right here?"

"No," Mother Cabrini said gently. "The world is only a small ball for the Missionary Sisters. See how the Infant Saviour holds it in His hands?"

SAINT FRANCES CABRINI

CHAPTER THIRTEEN

A FEW weeks later, as Pope Leo the Thirteenth listened to Mother Cabrini's report of her work, he experienced a variety of emotions. This frail little nun, through her few schools and one hospital in the New World, had actually brought hundreds of her fellow-countrymen back to the Church!

"Well done!" he exclaimed, placing his hand in blessing upon her head. "Well done, indeed!"

Mother Cabrini's heart beat fast. What a privilege to see and speak with the Vicar of Christ on earth! To know that her work was pleasing to him! Yet since there were countless claims upon the time and energy of this good friend, now eighty-two years old—

"No, Mother, don't be afraid of tiring me," said Pope Leo quickly, reading her thoughts. "Just tell me all about your plans for the future."

Mother Cabrini obeyed. It was good to be working among the Italian people in the United States, she said, but surely she ought to be helping other people as well? In Argentina and Brazil, for instance, where there was such a great need for up-to-date Catholic schools?

Pope Leo stared. "But you don't speak Spanish or Portuguese, Mother! And neither do any of your Sisters! How could you possibly manage such schools?"

Mother Cabrini laughed. "Your Holiness, didn't you send me to the United States when I knew scarcely a word of English?"

SAINT FRANCES CABRINI

CHAPTER FOURTEEN

POPE Leo was amused. Certainly this bright-eyed little religious had lost none of her sense of humor during her three years abroad. "I did, Mother," he chuckled. "And you obeyed gracefully. Yet I've never forgotten what you told Bishop Scalabrini when he made a similar request of you."

"Yes, Your Holiness? What did I say?"

" 'New York is too small a place for me.' Then, when he suggested the entire United States: 'No, for me the whole world is too small.' Ah, Mother, it does me good to find someone who's not afraid of hard work! By all means go to South America as soon as possible."

So Mother Cabrini began to lay plans for the Missionary Sisters of the Sacred Heart to start work in Argentina and Brazil. Yet never did she forget her responsibilities in the United States, and by 1899 had opened other schools in New York, as well as in Chicago, Scranton and Newark.

"There's no one with a better head for business than our Mother," the Missionary Sisters told one another admiringly. "She can hold her own with anyone."

"That's right. With lawyers or plumbers."

"With bankers or carpenters."

"Yet she's such a little thing! Not even five feet tall!"

"True, but she has the courage of a lion. It never pays to try to take advantage of her."

SAINT FRANCES CABRINI

CHAPTER FIFTEEN

ADMIRATION for Mother Cabrini increased as time went by. Her Missionary Sisters were needed in Paris, Madrid, London? Splendid! Even though funds were low and there seemed no way to arrange for a suitable convent, the Sisters would go. Or there was a lack of teachers and nurses in Denver, Seattle, Los Angeles? On to these cities at once! God would provide.

"We can do all things in Him Who strengthens us," Mother Cabrini cheerfully told her little family. "Nothing is ever to daunt you. You are to press on, not of yourselves, but under obedience. I have already learned that whenever I failed in any undertaking, it was because I trusted too much in my own powers. None of us will fail if we leave everything in the hands of God. Under Him, the question of what is possible and what is impossible ceases to have any meaning."

As a result of such good advice, the work of the Missionary Sisters grew and prospered on both sides of the Atlantic. And though Mother Cabrini would always love her native Italy, she finally made an important decision.

"The people of the United States have been wonderfully kind to me," she declared. "In gratitude, I'm going to become an American citizen."

So in 1909, in Seattle, Washington, fifty-nine-year-old Mary Frances Cabrini solemnly pledged allegiance to her adopted homeland—the United States of America!

SAINT FRANCES CABRINI

CHAPTER SIXTEEN

ALTHOUGH her friends were of all ages, Mother Cabrini was especially fond of children. Each Christmas, in her various schools and orphanages, she saw to it that everything possible was done to make them happy. Toys, games, candy, gay decorations—nothing was too much trouble. But in Chicago, in 1917, as Christmas week approached, the Sisters felt that the school children would have to go without candy that year. After all, World War I was raging in Europe, and times were hard.

"Oh, but we've got to have candy!" exclaimed Mother Cabrini. "Christmas wouldn't be Christmas without it!"

The Sisters smiled. Their sixty-seven-year-old superior (who had crossed the ocean twenty-five times and had opened sixty-seven houses of the Institute), was still just a child at heart!

"Very well, Mother," they said. "We'll get the candy and you can give it out."

But on December 22, in Chicago's Columbus Hospital, God called Mother Cabrini to Himself, so that the Christmas candy had to be distributed by someone else.

"Never mind," the neighborhood children told one another earnestly. "Mother Cabrini went straight to heaven when she died. Now she'll be able to help us more than ever."

True enough. So many miracles followed on Mother Cabrini's death that on July 7, 1946, Pope Pius the Twelfth declared her to be a canonized Saint of the Church—the first United States citizen ever to be so wonderfully honored.